MINI WALKS ON THE MESA

by
Ursula Cooper

Dorothy Harroun, Illustrator

Sunstone Press
Santa Fe, New Mexico

Library of Congress Cataloging in Publication Data:

Cooper, Ursula, 1918-
    Mini walks on the mesa / by Ursual Cooper ; Dorothy Harroun, illustrator. – 1st ed.
        p.   cm.
    ISBN: 0-86534-133-8 : $6.95
        1. Natural history – New Mexico – Juvenile literature.   2. Mesas – New Mexico
–Juvenile literature. I. Harroun, Dorothy. II. Title.
QH105.N6C66 1989
508.789–dc20   89-4448
                                                                                          CIP

Published in 1989 by SUNSTONE PRESS
                Post Office Box 2321
                Santa Fe, NM 87504-2321 / USA

DEDICATED TO
ALL PERSONS WHO LOVE GOOD ART,
DOGS — THE OUT-OF-DOORS
AND LIFE

New Mexico

SANTA FE ★

ALBUQUERQUE •

Canadian River

Gila River

GREETINGS!

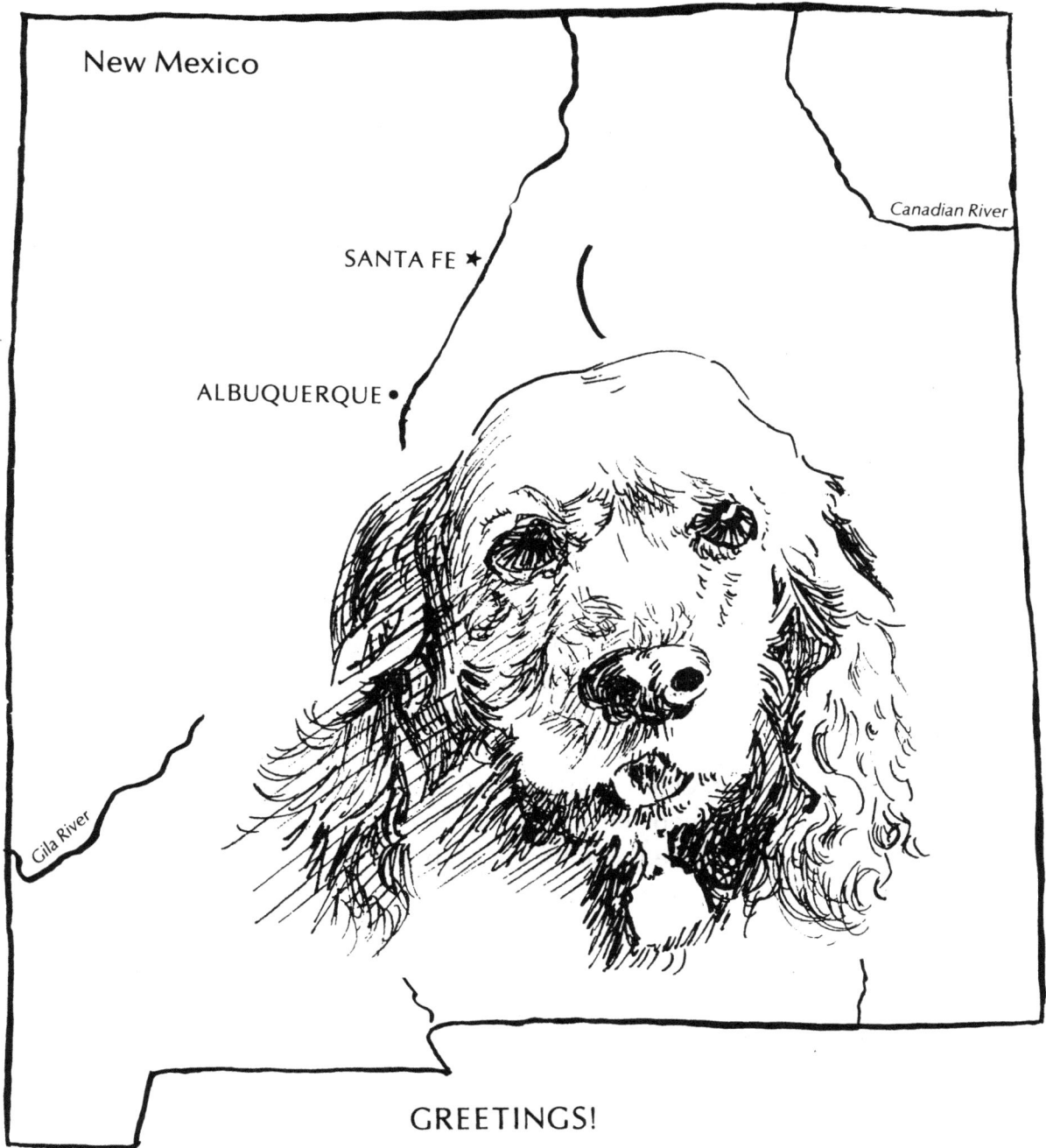

I am a four-year old, curious cocker spaniel. My name is Mini. I live in Albuquerque (New Mexico's largest city) with a retired couple. Happiness is meeting other dogs and people on our "Mini Walks" as we enjoy the out of doors. Mini Walks are the big excitement in my life. The ever-changing clouds, plants, trees, birds and animals keep my dog eyes busy. The scents and sounds send me off on many adverturous chases.

Every morning I wake up and send the moon spinning on its way, welcome the morning sun, and check the weather for the day. I run to get my leash and wait impatiently by the door to depart for another carefree, refreshing Mini Walk on the mesa.

My daily walks are taken in an area called Piedras Marcados, which translates in English to "marked rocks." This area is rich in nature and historical lore.

Wherever you look geographical formations are evident, such as the mountains, volcanoes, volcanic peaks, the high rocky escarpment, plains, mesa, and the fragmented ruins of Piedras Marcados arroyo.

Escarpment is a steep slope — a more or less extended line of cliffs. A mesa is a low, flat-topped mountain, or tableland, bounded on at least one side by a steep cliff called an escarpment. Mesa is the Spanish word for table. The west mesa, where I live, covers many miles.

The historical lore comes from Indians, Spanish and pioneers who used this area.

The marked rocks are called petroglyphs. They tell the story of Indians long ago. Most of these old glyphs (short for petroglyphs) were made by the Indians or Spanish between 400 and 1600 A.D.

The plants and animals, as you will read in the story, give me (Mini) great pain and pleasure.

From the flat-topped mesa we can see several mountain ranges, which include the Jemez, Sangre de Cristo, Sandia, and Manzano. Occasionally we get a glimpse of the volcanic peak, Mt. Taylor, 11,301 feet high. All of this scenic wonder makes a very dramatic backdrop for my Mini Walks.

Every walk is different. Sometimes my eyes catch glimpses of rabbits, and I dash off to chase them without success. One particular rabbit led me on a strenuous run until suddenly it disappeared. I snooped into an opening in the rocks hoping to find the rabbit. In the hole was a sleeping porcupine instead of my rabbit. The porcupine raised its quills, and I was lucky to escape with only a few in my hide. OUCH!

My friend Taco, a long-haired Mountain German Shepherd, wasn't so lucky. He went to the mesa without permission. Right after lunch I heard this howling, crying, barking, and no wonder, as Taco was full of porcupine quills. The neighbors took their hurting, crying, bleeding dog to the veterinarian. It took a long time to get all the quills out; Taco had to take shots and spend the night.

I only see porcupine in the area at the time of year when nearby houses have nice green gardens. Yes, we have found porcupine quills among the lettuce and zucchini at our house.

Porcupine are most active at night but may be seen during the day.

WEST MESA OF ALBUQUERQUE

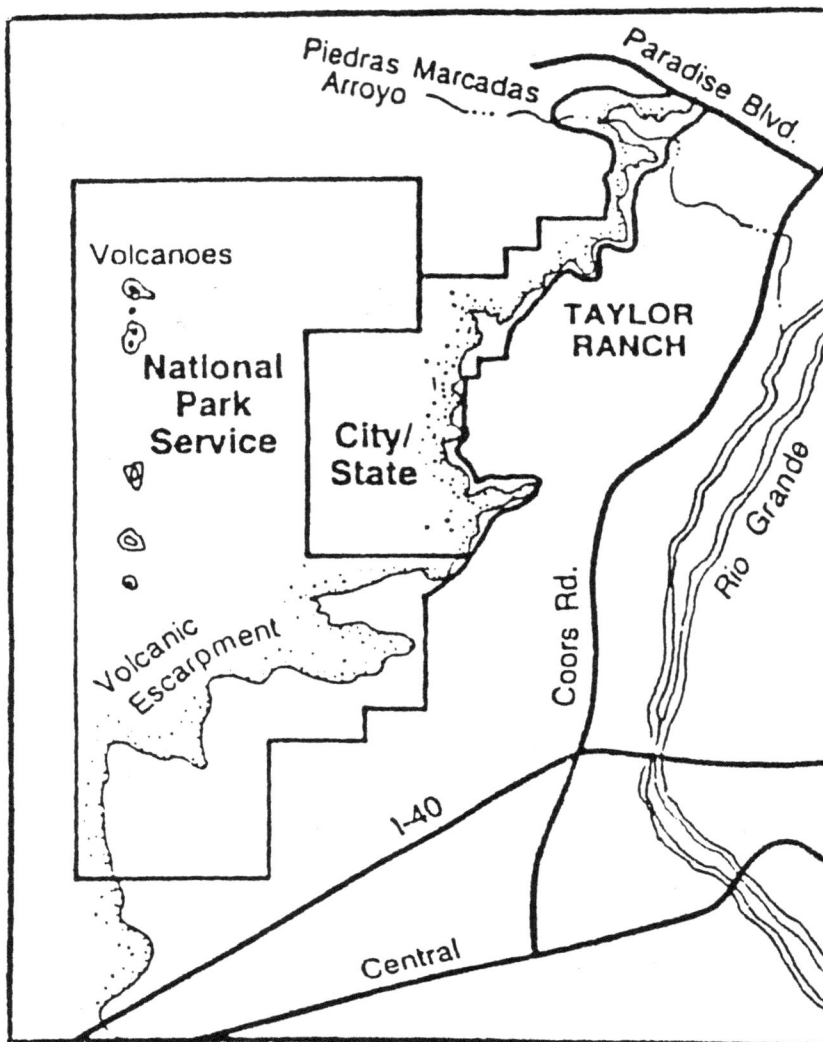

In the distance, five volcanic peaks estimated to be 190,000 years old, reside in silent splendor. From south to north, they are J.A., Black, Vulcan, Bond, and Butte. Vulcan is the tallest of the ancient cones, with an elevation of about 6,000 feet. The Albuquerque Open Space administration some day hopes to create a park around the volcanoes.

One late afternoon, black, threatening clouds gathered in the sky and formed a dense, grim curtain across the volcanoes. The storm clouds moved and settled down into the volcanic cones. The turbulant clouds lifted up and spun out long wispy trails from the ancient craters, which created the appearance of a volcanic eruption. Possibly the volcanoes looked something like that when they were young and smoldering. I made fast tracks to get home before the lightning and thunder started.

Down below the escarpment, I heard a symphony of chirping, chirp, cheep, chirp voices. There must be a covey of quail making their nests in the fourwing saltbush and sage on the slope. Some time later, I was held on my leash to keep me from scaring the new wobbly quail as they carefully followed their mother along the dusty road.

Sometimes on the mesa I run along the edge of a steep escarpment slope. Rough, black slabs; gray, bumpy volcanic boulders; basalt; brown rocks streaked with orange, green and yellow lichens splashed across them; and desert vegetation combine to form the incline under the escarpment rim. Along here you will find: turtles, rabbits, snakes, gophers, porcupines, skunks, chipmunks, beetles, butterflies, tarantulas, burrowing owls, quail, and many other creatures. One morning as I was sniffing around under the escarpment, much to my surprise I found a sleeping skunk. When he got up, he let loose with his not-too-pleasant spray, and when we got home they used a big, old-fashioned wash tub, soap, water and gallons of tomato juice. I was bathed, scrubbed, bathed again, and then thoroughly rebathed until all the skunk odor was gone. I couldn't stand my stink, so I was glad to be clean-smelling again.

My eyes notice that the mesa is very colorful as wild asters, indigo, small sunflowers, snakerroot, morning glories, and other flowers are blooming this fall. The wind sways the purple asters and small yellow sunflowers into rolling waves of color. Happiness is walking through these waves of color, breathing fresh air, watching the clouds drift along, and freedom to roam.

The rabbits go bounding in and out of the rocks, fourwinged saltbush, sage and indigo. I see a tail or an ear and off I go after a cottontail or a jackrabbit. They out run me every time.

The rabbits eat desert plants, and I have even seen them nibble on cacti. They seek resting places under the fourwinged saltbush.

The "swosh, swish" sounds from the big, bright, colorful balloon comes closer and closer. The noise starts me barking and pawing the ground, but when the balloonists are very close to us, one of the men yell "Good Morning! Guten Morgen! Buenos Dias! and Bon Jour!" As the gentle balloon drifts across the mesa, the other balloonist calls out "Good Bye! Guten Aben! Adois Amigos! Au Revoir!"

Many small neat holes have fresh mounds of dirt off to one side. For years I sniffed and barked at many of these holes but never scared out anything. For all my four years of life they have been a mystery to me. Finally I saw a small animal sitting outside its home. The gopher has a stocky hairy body, tail, small eyes and ears, and powerful digging claws. Soon it scurried away.

The grand-daughters were gleefully walking with us, as they do on all their visits and they said to us, "The pioneer French settlers gave the name gopher to various animals that burrow."

"The mounds of earth they throw out give away their homes."

"The burrows are hazardous traps for horses feet as well as other animals."

"Gophers have a lonely hard life and keep out of sight of their natural enemies which are birds of prey, snakes, and coyotes."

"Ocassionally they come above ground to gather food which they store for winter."

"Snakes and small animals appreciate finding and using the abandoned gopher holes."

Hi, stranger! What are you doing up on this mesa? One day a ferret was standing up on the rocks watching us as we passed by. I know that boys in our neighborhood have a ferret. Most likely it had sneaked out for a morning walk.

Early in my learning to walk and run on the mesa, I found out a few things about cactus plants; one is that cactus spines are sharp, hurt, and are hard to get out if they stick in you. To me, it doesn't matter if they are called Juniper Prickly Pear, Cliff Prickly Pear, Porcupine Prickly Pear, Tuberous Prickly Pear, Purple Fruited Prickly Pear, Desert Prickly Pear, or many other names — the spines hurt! I haven't been very close to the cacti for over two years.

I stand still, turn my head, pick up my ears, and look skyward. I hear many strange sounds and see the migrating birds. These birds are moving from one feeding ground to another. In the fall and spring thousands of birds, including snow geese, sandhill cranes, whooping cranes, Canadian geese, and a wide variety of ducks, fly over Albuquerque on their way to and from Bosque del Apache Wildlife Refuge near Socorro, New Mexico, and other points south.

Our mesa has a spectaucular view of the annual migrating flocks. From several points we can watch the migrating birds settle down on the banks of the Rio Grande to drink, eat and rest. This ritual has been going on for thousands of years.

All at once there is big flapping and rush of air. Could it be another hot-air ballon? Oh, no, these are the largest birds I have ever seen in my life. The whooping cranes seem to be the size of a small airplaine. They are hungry and eager to eat. I am very near the whoopig cranes and must stay quiet. What a rare day this one turned out to be!!!!

GREATER SANDHILL CRANES AND
WHOOPING CRANES MIGRATION

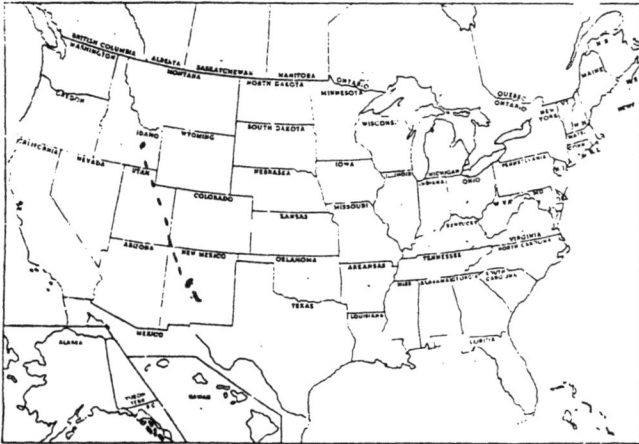

IDAHO
GRAY'S LAKE NATIONAL WILDLIFE REFUGE

NEW MEXICO
BOSQUE DEL APACHE NATIONAL WILDLIFE
REFUGE

One of the most exciting stories in the bird world is unfolding in Idaho's Gray National Wildlife Refuge in cooperation with New Mexico's Bosque del Apache National Wildlife Refuge.

The Idaho Gray Lake flock was started in 1975 by taking eggs from whooper nests in Canada and putting them in sandhill crane nests in the Idaho refuge. The sandhill cranes raised the whooping cranes. They migrate in the fall to Bosque del Apache, just south of Socorro. A massive effort has been put into the project to make it successful. It is believed the whooping crane mates for life.

The rare whooping crane is the tallest bird in North America. They have long necks and are about five feet tall. The wing span measures seven and one-half feet. The federal Endangered Species Act protects them.

Many more people visit the refuge when the whooping cranes are in residence.

It's a good thing I saw one on the mesa. — Min

OPEN SPACE
PRESERVE
NO MOTORIZED VEHICLES
BEYOND THIS SIGN

This open space land is designated for hiking, horseback riding, nature study, jogging, photography, pincicking.

PROHIBITED ACTIVITIES

Operation of motorized vehicles, hunting, removal of natural resouces, shooting, possession of glass containers, littering, firewood cutting, dumping, alcoholic beverages.

ARE PATROLLED

All violators will be prosecuted; fine of up to $300 or 60 days (Ordinance 23-1980).
HELP PROTECT YOUR NATURAL OPEN SPACE
City of Albuquerque
Parks and Recreation Department 766-7142

A long time ago when I was a puppy on a Mini Walk, a great, strong golden eagle sat silently upon a huge boulder. With piercing eyes, he followed my every movement. He circled above me and then returned to his majestic perch. He kept on watching me and finally soared in the sky. All at once he swooped down and tries to snatch me. Our whistling, shouting, and barking scared him away. Spreaking his seven-foot wings, the golden eagle flew toward the Sandia Mountains where eagles nest. I have seen eagles on other walks, but not often. They always look lonely and aloof, sitting high on their observation posts, searching, searching with their keen eyes.

In the middle of a tiny valley grows a lone, scrubby juniper tree. At different times various mesa inhabitants stop beneath its humble branches to make a home or rest a while.

I was quietly sniffing along and whee! Suddenly a hawk flew up from the ground and startled both of us. The commotion scared out a cottontail rabbit, which the hawk took after, I ran in the opposite direction. Most hawks fly very fast as they chase their prey.

In an abandoned gopher hole under the same juniper tree, a burrowing owl set up housekeeping. The owl has good daytime vision and works hard to find rodents, insects and lizards to feed its young. I was put on a leash and not allowed to get close to the babies.

On our Mini Walks we stop and enjoy looking at petroglyphs. These drawings tell of Indian life that centered on nature's gifts of the sun, moon, stars, mountains, rain; earth's stories, plants, animals; and the supreme gift of man's intelligence.

Matthew F. Schmader of the University of New Mexico, Office of Contract Archaeology, docomented 3,600 petroglyphs (ancient Indian rock etchings). There are about 15,000 petroglyphs along the steep, rocky slopes of the escarpment. They tell of the creation of earth and the plants, animals, birds and people living at the time.

Talking about and sketching the petroglyphs takes a long time. When possible, I dig a hole, curl up and rest.

The group discusses what the experts are learning about cultural life, ceremonies, hunting, agriculture, and other important messages from the past.

The oldest petroglyphs (pictures) have a worn, dark-mellow, antique appearnce called patina. Age and weathering create the patina, and five hundred years does not produce very much. Look at several petroglyphs and soon you will see the difference between the old and new pictures. Some defacements are made as recent as yesterday, and they look all rough and ugly. All of this unnecessary marking spoils the old petroglyphs for study.

A concentrated effort by New Mexicans and others has been mounted to create a national monument that would provide protection for the petroglyphs and give many visitors enjoyment. Ike Eastvold, a writer and president of The Friends of the Albuquerque Petroglyphs, has helped co-ordinate a massive work force to establish The Petroglyph National Monument.

All I know of the coyote is his plaintive high-pitched wails. I have never seen one up close. My dog instincts respond to his mournful song, and I know that we are somehow kindred relatives. His serenade sounds lonely, restless and alone. The coyote is chiefly nocturnal, but may be about at any time.

The day is winding down as the sun sets, the birds continue on their migration, the yaps of the coyote fade into the distance, and my day is about complete. Home for supper, sleep, and tomorrow is another Mini Walk on the Mesa.

www.ingramcontent.com/pod-product-compliance
Lightning Source LLC
Chambersburg PA
CBHW081420090426
42738CB00017B/3432